POEMS FROM SPIRIT

A COLLECTION OF POEMS TO UPLIFT THE SOUL

BY

MINISTER LYN HARRÉ

PUBLISHED BY JM LM PUBLICATIONS, 2025

FOR ALL CORRESPONDENCE:

JM LM PUBLICATIONS

8 MATIPO CRESCENT

HAMILTON 3200

NEW ZEALAND

EMAIL: justin@fingersoffire.com

ABOUT THE AUTHOR

Lyn Harré is a retired Spiritualist Minister, Celebrant and Healer who has served in Hamilton, New Zealand. for many years.

Lyn has written poetry all her life as did her Mother and Grandfather.

Spirit gives her the right words at the right time to help her and others on their Spiritual journey as they walk the way together.

By sharing her poems Lyn hopes you will be uplifted in your soul by the given words from Spirit.

TABLE OF CONTENTS

A MESSAGE FROM LYN

It is a privilege to share my thoughts with you that I have been blessed by Spirit, to receive.

May I encourage those of you who have also been given this gift by Spirit to use this medium of print to share your talent.

Listen to the stillness and quietness for your guidance.

Thanks for reading

Love and light

Lyn

Friendship must be a bond of two hearts

and not just one,

For when it is only one-sided,

true to course, it will not run

If only one makes the effort to keep the friendship alive,

failure it will constantly meet, however hard it may

strive

For friendship based by one, cannot meet the test,

of many ups and downs and yet remain the best

Two hearts that beat as one, will ultimately share,

the love of the friendship that will always be there

For it is not by one alone that friendship comes to be,

it is by two hearts combined together in perfect
harmony

No words should ever be needed, no dialogue on end,

For all the wonderful meanings in the world,

are contained in the one word 'FRIEND'

We only briefly touch each other's lives, be they foolish
or worldly wise

An instant spark of knowingness - triggers a memory of
happiness

And one recalls a past attraction,

of deep desires and satisfaction

But it is only brief and the Spirit knows - that as quickly
as it came,

it also goes

For a life is only a brief sojourn,

to enhance our nature since we were born

Briefly touching another soul, to make them better, to
make them whole

For this is the way the young soul learns, to travel the
Earth in between sojourns

to reconnect for a specific reason, to teach the soul its
many seasons

Yes only briefly my light touches yours, before we go back to familiar shores

Only briefly will you know my name, and remember why I came

The young soul learns not to fret, for the times on Earth are not over yet,

For magic is waiting in so many places, and the young soul rejoices at many new faces

For the magic that each soul brings, gives the new soul its Angel wings,

Home it goes to earn its rest,

For each soul it touched it passed the test

Have you ever wondered why I know you so well?

Would you believe me if I told you I can tell,

I can tell the moment that I look in your eyes, your soul

I truly know, and instantly recogníze

You cannot hide the truth of your soul light so bright, It

shines from deep within like a candle in the night

I cannot run away from those I've met before, They

enter my heart so softly that I surely can't ignore

They come to reassure me that I am never on my own,

My soul recognises the familiarity known

Speaking is never necessary when these ones touch my

soul, with just a little look, they make me completely

whole

You may say this is madness of a very strange kind, and

yes I've been told I might have lost my mind,

But I know my truth ínside me and I do not doubt at all,

because the soul never lies and always responds to the

true call

You may feel the connection, I'm sure that you do, so

just enjoy the magic, if these things happen to you!

I have a problem, my friend said, could you listen if you cared

My problem weighs heavy on my mind, for peace and freedom I cannot find

So I took the tíme to hold her hand,

to soothe her mind and to help her stand

Help her stand in her own light once more, and on this problem,

close the door

We talked and talked to the wee small hours,

We shared our friendship - that was ours

And suddenly the answer appeared!

We laughed and cried and shed some tears

You know it did not take very long, to help my friend

sing her song, Sing her song of joy once more,

It was only caring that she longed for

So remember this when a friend needs an ear,

the main ingredient is that you care

To hold a hand, to give some time,

what a privilege, yours and mine

To help someone the cost is small,

to help them feel ten feet tall

My friend, life changes from beginning to end,

things are never what they seem

Appearing to us like phantom dreams

Our days and nights merge into one

From early dawn to setting sun

Each one of us playing a role,

Trying to be sane and totally whole

Caught up in life and all that that may be,

Caught up with who we are meant to be

Our roles so often changing face,

Bearing sorrow or moments of grace

Taking part in this drama called life,

Embracing moments of joy and strife

One day laughing and as free as air,

One day being as devil may care

But another day testing us beyond our strength,

Having to go from length to length

Being asked to do our best, so we can pass the test,

Pass the test of what others expect,

For the lessons are not over yet

But mixed in the moments of every day,

Our personal ethics will show the way,

And guide us to the place of rest,

Content to know we did our best

Good Morning my dear one who do you see?

Can you please speak to me, because I am still ME

Although my words maybe funny and come out wrong,

I'm still trying to sing my own song

In my presently mixed up frame of mind,

I'm still ME deep down you will find

And although I cannot remember your name,

apart from my problem, I'm still the same

I'm just a bit lost in this unusual place,

And I'm sure you can see it on my face

I try so hard to sort the words in my head,

But they come out wrong, and muddled instead

I may have wandered around the place,

Looking for your familiar face,

While you were there all the time for me,

But in MY memory, I can no longer see

I hear and feel things that I cannot express,

And I'm trying to find that happiness,

That I always feel when you hold me tight,

And comfort me each day and night

I know this journey may be hard and long,

And I have forgotten the words to my song,

But please have patience and you will see,

in some fleeting moments, I am still ME

The touch of your hand, and your lips on mine,

take me back to a special time,

And in that moment of granted grace,I can remember

your loving face,

how it was before this happened to me, your own true

love I will always be

Walk with me while I age, upon this earth-bound stage

keep in step with my weakened gait,

share time with me before it is too late

Walk with me down through the many years,

please share with me the laughter and tears

and if I cry far more than my share,

in your kindness please wipe away each tear

Walk with me through each passing phase,

in the sunshine of our days,

For every day is a jewel in disguise,

when I see your smiling eyes

Walk with me while I age,

help me to turn every page,

Every page that I may turn with you,

helps a dream to come true

Walk with me and take my hand,

share with me your dreams and plans

Walk with me with your youthful step,

help me to remember, should I forget

Walk with me friend, partner, or lover,

walk with me doctor, nurse,

or other

Walk with me as you see me age,

help me to prepare for my final stage

Walk with me as I walk with you,

and know I love you for being true

Passing like ships in the night, that briefly recognize

each other by a blast on their horn

Passing by on a calm sea, sometimes a storm,

Passing by at midnight, sometimes dawn

How little we know about each other,

how little time there is to share,

Meeting ever so briefly, taking time to care

Moving in and out on the sea of daily life,

Passing by most things, not giving in to strife

The waves of personal experience alone controlled by

time,

No feelings or emotions expressed by yours and mine

Ships that come and go with a cargo of this and that,

Ships that pass each other, but have no time to chat

Upon the sea of life we get tossed to and fro,

The overwhelming waves always seem to know -

that we have little control over the compass of our

lives,

Although for perfection and order we constantly strive

We plot our own little voyage and map our own little

way,

We pass by each other silently, not lingering to stay

Yes as ships in the night upon the sea of change,

I look for your flag, but you are out of range,

I do not hear your whistle, neither hear your horn,

you pass me by in silence in the early morn

Ships in the night along our pathway we go,

to reach our destination that our own compass shows!

A summers day, a frosty morn,

Broken ice on the mown lawn

A little sparrow still sings his song,

He will sing all day long

A loyal cat purring on my knee,

He just wants to be with me,

He too sings his song,

No matter what is right or wrong

A mug of hot coffee or tea,

and toast with lovely honey,

Eaten slowly to the ticking clock,

All measured by the pills I nearly forgot!

A friend who rings to ask how I am,

Am I well or in a jam?

Such a delight to hear her say,

I will come to see you today!

My nice warm shower that keeps me clean,

and with the soap I am never mean

And as I rug up nice and warm,

to be protected by winter's storm

Some music that calms my racing heart,

and gives me courage for a better start

To let me know I can be strong or weak,

to say my prayers and my Lord to seek

Every day has a bonus unseen,

hidden delights that have never been

To open my eyes and my heart as well,

these are the joys of them I can tell

HE'S MY CAT

He's my cat - but he's more than that

He's my best friend,

On him I depend,

He gives his love so cheerfully,

Especially when he's on my knee,

He just purrs and looks up to me

He's my cat - but he's more than that,

He takes the sting out of being lonely,

He gives his love to me only

He welcomes me with a smooch and a purr

He lets me stroke his soft warm fur

He's my cat - but he's more than that,

He fills my days with his playful ways,

And my nights with company

He stills my heart when I am down,

He just knows when to come around

He looks at me with love in his eyes,

He to me is very wise

He's my cat - but he's more than that

My soul companion for sure

In loving memory of KittyKat

Your actions affect mine,

down the years all through time

If your actions reflect on me,

do they help to make me see?

A negative or a positive point of view,

depending on how I see you

If the action that you take is grim,

where does that put me in?

How do I justify the way you make your call,

Will it help me to rise or fall

But by your actions the truth must first take place,

This will be shown ín your honest face

Then I will know that your actions are pure,

and down the years will endure

How many tímes do the actions you express,

give me sorrow or happiness

But I cannot question the role that you play,

You bid me to follow, or run away

It takes courage to believe that you will do no harm,

And I must trust that inner calm,

That I see in you as the years roll by,

Steadfast and true with a steady eye

Your actions are pure, your intention true,

No wonder I keep my faith in you!

I like the stillness of the night,

When all others have gone from sight

I like the quietness the end of day brings,

I can almost hear Angel wings

I can feel the peace, in my quiet soul,

I feel content, and once more whole

For in this moment of peaceful serene,

My God is here, as has always been

I came across a little stumbling block
that stood in my way,
Why have you come to stop me, I did say
It looked at me with unknown eyes never seen before,
And spoke to me in an unknown tongue I did not know
for sure
I asked again in an anxious way who are you and of
what kin
It replied to me in a funny voice, I am known as Lyn

I said, I do not know who you are,
although I recognize my name,
it looked at me with sad sad eyes and said,
that is why I came

You had to have this stumbling block that carries your
own name,
You had to look with open eyes as to why to you I came
The path has not gone right for you,
it has stopped you in your tracks,
The stumbling block is there for you so you would
somehow get back

I really needed to search this block that had suddenly appeared,
I looked deep down in my heart and went back many years
I looked at all my records of my life up to today,
I looked with an open heart to see what it would say
And then I saw the path again, that I very nearly missed,
It suddenly appeared again from out of all the mist

I saw the way I nearly went when searching through my life,
So I quickly got back on the track to avoid any more strife

I want to thank you stumbling block for helping me to see,
To open my eyes, to open my heart, and to get back to the real me

You never gave me your company,

nor did you stay awhile,

I waited so long to see you,

but you just passed me by

The hours and days so lonely, the nights so lonely too,

I cried upon my pillow with sad thoughts

of you

How can you be so uncaring, so mean,

and so blind,

When I really thought that a treasure I did find

Just two little hours for you to say good day,

but no you had no time and just went on your way

You will never really know how hurt you made me feel,

I try to act normal, but my emotions I conceal

I never asked for much, just your warm loving smile,

but you never had the time to be with me awhile

So maybe one day when you grow old like me,

you will reflect on what you could have done,

to give me some company

The years pass quickly, as do the falling leaves,

the time on Earth many memories leave,

the happenings to us remain in our mindseye,

and the times we lived go fastly by

A brief flirtation, an honest love,

all come to us from those we love,

and even though the years have passed,

we still remember they still do last

In our private book of special things,

The heart recalls and the memory clings,

And takes us back to that special time,

When either young or old the memory to find

Nothing is ever lost from the years spent below,

You will keep the memories, and you will always know

Even through the darkness when the mind will go

astray,

An instant time of recall will come to you on some

special day

So gather all the memories and the love given to you

Celebrate each happening because it is really true,

That we do not know the number of our days here on

earth,

Live each moment fully and share it for what it's worth

For the years pass quickly as do the falling leaves

So enhance every happening,

before your spirit leaves

Thank you for the little things that grace my life each
day
the friendly hello, the super smiles,
the hugs you give along the way

The courteous way you speak to me,
the listening ear you lend, your concern for my
wellbeing, on your friendship I can depend

The kindness you extend to me,
in a hundred little ways
they all add up to make my life so blessed in many ways

A kindred soul, a fellow companion, on this journey
that we share
a helping hand in times of sorrow,
to know you will be there

Thank you Lord for gracious souls,

who walk along with me

they take away the loneliness,

and open my eyes to see

They come so softly into my heart

and help my soul to sing

they bring their love, their healing balm,

as beautiful as Angel's wings

So thank you for the little blessings,

that come with little things,

but add so much joy and pleasure,

to make our hearts truly sing

Youth has come, and youth has gone,

but left me with a lovely song

the paths I took to get me there,

but now I am wondering where is here

It seems only yesterday I was so young,

I had lots of drama but mostly fun

The love I received from family and kin

Showed the place I fitted in

As the years moved swiftly by,

I lost some friends who went and died

They left a hollow in my heart and mind,

and I wondered why I was left behind

But a tender and loving heavenly father,

Could see that I had to go farther

To meet others likeminded like me

who opened up my spiritual eyes to see

So the path goes on with these loving souls,

Each one helping to make me whole

Giving me their wisdom too

new beginnings from each day anew

How blessed am I to have this treasure,

my heart overflows beyond all measure

My song of praise will last my days,

in youth and age, forever always

We all come to Earth with music in our souls

some remember it now, others when time unfolds

We are each given a special song,

to play during our life,

with tones, beats and melody,

that should create harmony, not strife

If you quaver when the notes don't hit the right place,

Or your melody goes wrong and mistakes you can't

face,

Then you need to get back your rhythm and your own

true beat,

So you can go on singing with those other notes you

meet

Don't forget to pause as you join in the chorus too,

Others may be out of tune and are counting on you

You may meet others whose beat is too fast

But first remember it is them that have to last,

You would not fit to their tune, for you know your own pace,

Be content to know you have your own special place

The music in your soul was meant for you alone,

To share with others on this Earth before you go home

So join in the chorus with those who sing their song,

Create that lovely harmony and learn to sing along!

With a song in my heart I came to Earth,
to sing my song for what it is worth
From spheres of Heaven to lower below,
to sing my song to those I know

With a song for those who walked with me,
in Green Valleys and beside the Sea
Those I knew and those yet to meet,
those companion souls - so very sweet

With a song for me and a song for you,
the music given to the beat so true
A melody given for each one I meet,
in harmony and in tune when we did greet
Each one of us must sing our own song,
And find the place where we belong

High or low notes don't matter much,

It is the tune within the vibrant touch,

That brings the harmony, that expresses the soul,

to sing the song to make one whole

With a song in my heart I will sing with praise,

along with others to the end of my days

When I am gone from this place called Earth,

I hope you will say that I had some worth,

Was worthy of being a decent soul,

A kind person on the whole

I tried my best to be loving and kind,

and hoped that in my family they did find,

that as a sister, Aunt and a friend to all,

I tried to answer when you did call

One never knows how they are perceived,

not always warmly well received

But still part of a family we are,

always reaching for that far off star

To gather the lost ones, the sad and lonely,

to offer compassion, to be warm and homely

Warm and giving to those who are broken,

this never needs words to be spoken

A gentle touch, a glance of love,

Is all that's needed as soft as a dove

I hope you found my heart was warm,

And that I sheltered you from the occasional storm,

For then I will go to my final rest,

and know in my heart I tried my best

We are all connected to a family, each one of us for
sure,
Some of us fit in, others only endure,
Endure to find their place among the family strong,
some of us fit in, others wonder what went wrong

Each one of us is different in their own peculiar way,
we wonder why on Earth, in this family we came to stay
We kind of look alike our faces sometimes show,
the family connection to the Mum and Dad you know

But really down deep inside we are really on our own,
from babyhood to age we make our character known
We may look a like as people will truly say,
but I am NOT my sister, I'm ME in every way!

No matter where you fit in, the beginning or the end,
each one of us is different on that you can depend
No matter what the plan to make you conform,
you are your own true self since the moment you were
born

Yes you planned to join that family, you chose it from above,
you knew you would be welcome, and very much loved
and in spite of being different, you chose that family true,
your character was needed, and they needed you

Because each one makes a mix of good points and bad,
each one of us is needed to bring happy and sometimes sad,
Because the family that you chose was surely the right one,
and there you will remain till your time on Earth is done

They call me when someone dies,

and loses the light from their eyes

They call me and ask for prayers,

as they look on with stoney stares

They call me to tell them what to do,

for most of them this is something new

They call me to offer my compassion and care,

while in hopelessness they remain standing there

Such is the duty of a serving soul,

we go to help, to perform our role

Our role of minister, doctor or friend,

to be there for them, on us they depend

We do not flinch or deny what is asked,

for the one gone home has finished their task,

And as we serve to those left behind,

We offer our service giving peace of mind

The face of death is no stranger to me,

it is all part of who I chose to be,

To be there for those who can not function,

while as a minister we prepare to unction

To offer the soul now anointing with oil,

perfect peace and release from toil

The face of death is no stranger to me,

for in the light of God true beauty you see,

That someone once loved has now gone to rest,

Leaving those who serve to now do their best,

To offer their service with intention true,

this is the role played by me and you

I hope you have enjoyed these pages.

It was a pleasure for me to write these words with the help of Spirit.

I hope that you have gained some inspiration from these words and that they make a difference to your life.

Lyn

www.ingramcontent.com/pod-product-compliance
Lightning Source LLC
Chambersburg PA
CBHW051234090426
42740CB00001B/13